Totally Awesome Facts to Blow Your Curious Mind

An Amusing Collection of 525 Random Facts on Just About Everything

By Ian Hall

CONTENTS

Introduction

When I was 10 years old, my parents presented me a copy of Ripley's Believe It or Not. Ever since that time, I have been an avid collector of odd facts, just plain facts, and unusual items that appear in newspapers and magazines. In this book, I would like to share with you some of the interesting facts I have collected.

This book is full of facts. Some of them will amaze you, some will surprise you and some will start you thinking, so that you discover more about the subject. Hopefully, after reading this book you will be a cleverer person than when you started.

No matter what your curiosity or particular interest, you will easily be able to learn hundreds and hundreds of facts on dozens of subjects - from business and economics to health and the human body, from entertainment to politics to sports. There are 525 random facts here that cover far ranging topics.

Ian
Hall

FACTS 1 - 104

1. In 1876 Alexander Graham Bell made the first telephone call ever. Saying, "Mr. Watson, come here – I want to see you," he called his assistant who was in an adjacent room.

2. "Bookkeeper" and "bookkeeping" are the only words in the English language having three sets of double letters in a row.

3. You pee enough in your lifetime to fill a small swimming pool. That's equivalent to 10,000 gallons.

4. Bubbles were used as a toy almost 400 years ago. Flemish paintings from the 17th century showed children using clay pipes to blow bubbles.

5. Horses never breathe through their mouths, except in emergencies.

6. It appears that during his lifetime, famed 20th-century painter Vincent van Gogh sold only one painting.

7. The onion is the most popular vegetable in the world.

8. Camels can survive for many days without food or water. In their humps, they store a lot of fat. A camel that has a sagging hump is obviously hungry! They don't lose water from their body. Their urine is solid crystals, and they do not sweat.

9. We refer to a collection of bananas as a hand! A

single is called a finger.

10. The first food eaten in space by an American astronaut was applesauce.

11. A sea otter has the thickest fur of any animal. Its skin contains as many hairs on 0.16 square inch of its skin as we have on our whole head – 150,000.

12. After being diagnosed with blood poisoning on March 14, 1942, Anne Miller was given a tablespoon of penicillin, which was one half of the entire stockpile of the antibiotic in the United States.

13. Some tropical catfish eat their food while swimming upside down.

14. Mona Lisa, the well-known painting, has a mailbox of her own and received plenty of flowers and love letters from admirers.

15. People from western China, Mongolia, and Tibet add salt to their tea instead of sugar.

16. Venus is called "Earth's evil twin" because, despite being similar in size, it is hostile to life.

17. The reason those guys in commercial disclaimer voices speak so quickly is because they digitally eliminate the spaces between words and syllables in addition to speaking hastily.

18. Although matinees are always held in the afternoon, the name "matinee" is derived from the French word meaning "morning."

19. Approximately 80,000 km (50,000 miles) of veins and capillaries make up the human body.

20. Frozen sea water contains only around one-tenth of the salt content found in liquid seawater because most of the salt separates from the water when it becomes frozen. Because it contains so much salt, seawater freezes at around 28.4 degrees Fahrenheit.

21. The human kidneys are made up of around 280 miles of tiny tubes.

22. Gerbils that live in deserts never need to drink because they obtain all the moisture they require form the overnight dew on their food.

23. Spiders, lobsters, and snails have blue blood due to the presence of hemocyanin, which contains copper.

24. There is no known smaller unit of time than Planck time. It's 0.00000000000 00000000000000000000000000001 second.

25. Manila in the Philippines is the most crowded megacity with almost 41,000 people per square kilometer — 12 times as many as in Los Angeles!

26. Only a few animals, including humans, dolphins, big apes, magpies, and elephants, can identify themselves in the mirror.

27. A survivor of the titanic disaster also managed to survive the sinking of the Empress of Ireland 2 years later!

28. Australian lyrebirds can imitate almost any sound, such as those made by phones, chainsaws, cat alarms, barking dogs, and crying babies.

29. Every day, plants use sunlight to create energy equivalent to six times the entire power consumption of human civilization.

30. The smile is the only gesture which man does not share with other animals.

31. The shortest presidency in the world history was by president Pedro Paredes of Mexico who held office for less than one hour on February 19, 1913.

32. It was Thomas Paine, author of common sense, who first used the words "The United States of America."

33. Every day, more than 75 million meteors enter the earth's atmosphere, but most are only the size of a pin head.

34. Sauroposeidon proteles, the tallest known dinosaur, was taller than a six story building.

35. The Sahara in Africa is by far the largest desert in the world. The Sahara is larger than the combined area of the next four largest deserts. It is almost the same size as the whole of Europe.

36. Ancient Egyptians firmly believed that a person's soul was located in the heart.

37. There are claimed to be more ghosts per square kilometer in England than in any other country on earth.

38. There is only one vowel in "indivisibilty," and it occurs six times.

39. A study conducted in Austria found that kids between the ages of 11 and 16 who have pets are more popular at school and have more friends visit them at home.

40. Tv was banned in Iceland from 1966 to 1987 to encourage people to get out and socialise more.

41. According to statistics from Facebook more couples break up in the spring and the two weeks leading up to Christmas than at any other time of the year.

42. Earth loses around 100,000 tonnes of mass annually as a result of gases like helium and hydrogen escaping the atmosphere.

43. In Japanese culture, shaving one's head is a common way to publicly apologise or admit a failure.

44. The sixth president of the united states, John Quincy Adams, would swim naked in the Potomac river every day at five in the morning.

45. The testicles of the octopus are located in its head.

46. The South African railway once employed a baboon, named Jack as a signalman. Jack served for eight years without making a single mistake.

47. Jahangir, a seventeenth-century Indian Mughal ruler, had 5,000 women in his harem and 1,000 young boys. Moreover, he owned 12,000 elephants.

48. The retina of the dragonfly's eye is covered with over 30,000 lenses, so it sees many, many images where we only see one.

49. In 1800, there were only fifty cities on earth with a population of more than 100,000.

50. Sloths only poop once a week; they also must do it on the ground, making them an ideal target for predators. A sloth can release all of its waste in a single push, losing up to one-third of its total weight in the process. Once they have completed their task, they cover up the small hole they dug and return to the trees.

51. You have no control over some of your muscles! These are called involuntary muscles, which the body needs for functions such as breathing and food digestion.

52. An average man will shave for 3,500 hours in his lifetime. In this time, he removes about 30 ft of whiskers off his face.

53. Chewing gum immediately after listening to a catchy song reduces the likelihood to get the song stuck in your head.

54. The most recognisable smell from outer space is that of burning hydrocarbons, such as gunpowder, diesel, and barbecue sauce. Astronauts have reported smelling burned or fried steak after a spacewalk.

55. The human brain stops growing at the age of eighteen.

56. The male silkworm moth has the keenest sense of smell in the natural world. It can detect the sex signals of a female 6.8 miles away!

57. Dubai has 30,000 construction cranes, or 24% of all construction cranes in the world.

58. If the water from all the oceans in the world evaporated, the salt that remained would form a cube 165 miles on each side.

59. About 540 peanuts are needed to make a small jar of peanut butter.

60. A walrus walks on its teeth. It uses its long tusks to get out of the sea and move along the ground.

61. The amazon river is so powerful that fresh water can be taken from the sea and drunk 160km (100 miles) from the river mouth.

62. If you ate the liver of a polar bear, you would get vitamin a poisoning and could die. Polar bears have 50-60 times the normal human levels of vitamin A in their liver, and it is about three times the maximum amount that humans should be able to consume.

63. Some midges beat their wings at up to 62,760 times a minute. Not surprisingly, they have a very short lifespan.

64. Spiders avoid getting trapped in their own webs because they cover themselves with a greasy anti-silk film.

65. The African red-billed queleas are the most abundant birds in the world. It may take up to five hours for a flock to pass overhead.

66. Thiomargarita namibiensis, the largest bacteria in existence, can be seen without the aid of a microscope by the human eye.

67. The T. Rex roar in Jurassic Park (1993) is created by blending the sounds of a baby elephant's blast with growls from an alligator and shrieks from a tiger.

68. In your dreams, you don't create new faces; instead, they are all faces of people you've encountered before!

69. The hormone responsible for your growth is produced exclusively during sleep, so if you aim to become taller, it's important to go to bed when you're told!

70. Ten percent of perfume sales in Britain take place at Heathrow airport.

71. The pentagon, the headquarters of the us defense department, has approximately 174 miles of corridors in total length.

72. The world's longest place name belongs to a hill in New Zealand, known as taumatawhakatangihangakoauotamateaturipukakapikimaungahoronukupokaiwhenuakitanataha. Try saying it three times fast!

73. The average person will spend two weeks of their lifetime waiting for a traffic light to turn green.

74. Pee has fewer bacteria and microorganisms compared to the water from your kitchen faucet.

75. From the early 1700s to 1862, soap was seen as a frivolous luxury for the British aristocracy, and a tax was levied on those who used it in England.

76. The longest film ever made premiered in 1970, lasting 48 hours, and was titled the longest, most meaningless movie in the world.

77. In 1975, Mrs. Gwen Mathewman from West Yorkshire knitted 885 garments, using 29,852 kilograms of wool, which is equal to the fleece of 85 sheep.

78. Bluey, an Australian cattle dog, holds the title of the world's oldest dog, living to the age of 29.

79. While sucking your blood, mosquitoes also pee on you. Mosquitoes need to eliminate excess fluid and salts as they suck blood, so they urinate to keep their fluid and salt levels in balance.

80. Every year, a zoo in Tokyo closes for two months to allow the animals to rest and have a break from visitors.

81. On average, driving 50 miles in a car gives a person a one-in-a-million chance of being involved in a fatal accident.

82. A Boeing 767 aircraft is constructed from 3,100,000 distinct parts.

83. Cats spend approximately one-third of their waking hours cleaning their fur. Their licking behavior is primarily aimed at removing human scents acquired through interactions with their owners.

84. Your feet contain 52 bones, which make up approximately one-fourth of all the bones in your entire body.

85. The hummingbird has the largest brain proportionate to its body size in the bird kingdom, with its tiny brain accounting for 4.2 percent of its body weight.

86. Zero is the only number that cannot be represented by roman numerals.

87. There is uncertainty about whether the Mexican chihuahua should be classified as a dog or considered a type of rodent.

88. Google was initially called "backrub," because the search engine utilized backlinks to determine the importance of a website.

89. In the English language, there are six words containing the letter combination "uu": muumuu, vacuum, continuum, duumvirate, duumvir, and residuum.

90. There is a tribe in South America known as the "Tukano tribe" where the men are required to marry outside of their language group to ensure that children will be born into a multilingual household.

91. From 1870 to 1891, the postal system in Afghanistan required postmasters to cancel letters by biting off a corner of the stamp.

92. Some cells in our body are incredibly small that the head of a pin could hold as many as 200,000 of them.

93. It can take a saguaro cactus 10 years to grow by just one inch (2.5 cm).

94. A gazelle that is two days old can run at a speed of 96 km/h (60 mph) and surpass the running pace of a full-grown racehorse.

95. Leonardo da Vinci's Mona Liga was originally purchased by King Francis I of France with the intention of hanging it in his bathroom.

96. A person sneezing was the first thing Thomas Edison filmed with his movie camera.

97. Medieval People drilled holes in people's skulls to relieve headaches or ward off evil spirits.

98. A human-piloted rocket can reach the moon in less time than it took a stagecoach to traverse the length of England.

99. Somalia once issued a coin in the shape of a guitar!

100. Carnivorous plants that consume the largest prey belong to the Nepenthacae family. These plants, found in the Asian rainforest, can digest frogs, birds, and rats.

101. New Zealanders consume the highest amount of ice cream in the world, averaging 7.5 gallons (28.4 liters) per person each year!

102. In 1933, a man purchased the coat, vest, and pants worn by Abraham Lincoln on the night he was assassinated for $6,500.

103. Sheep have the ability to detect the faces of other sheep similar to how humans do. Researchers claim that they can remember up to 50 sheep faces.

104. In ancient Persian funerals, mourners used to collect and store their tears in bottles due to the widely held belief that human tears were excellent remedies for various conditions.

FACTS 105 – 209

105. The top speed a giant tortoise can crawl is around 5 yards a minute. A rabbit can cover the same distance in under half a second.

106. Our galaxy, the Milky Way, is believed to contain 200 to 400 billion stars.

107. You can't sink in the Dead Sea. The high salt content in the water offers significant buoyancy, allowing people to float with ease.

108. At least 9 million other people around the world share the same birthday as you.

109. In the 1966 World Cup final, Geoff Hurst scored three goals - one with a header, one with his left foot and one with his right foot. It was a record.

110. The distance between the wingtips of a Boeing 747 is longer than the first flight made by the Wright Brothers.

111. If you count without interruption, it would take approximately eleven and a half days to reach one million seconds and 32 years to reach one billion seconds.

112. The most active muscles in the human body are in the eyes; it is estimated that they move 100,000 times every day.

113. The longest war in world history lasted for 116 years. It was between England and France and started in 1337.

114. International Airport at Chicago is incredibly busy that on an average around 85 aeroplanes land and take-off from this airport every hour.

115. About 400 miles beneath the Earth's crust, there exists a vast reservoir of water, with a volume three times that of all the oceans combined. This water is contained within a mineral known as ringwoodite.

116. The Sultan of Brunei owns a palace with more than 1800 rooms which is probably the largest palace in the world.

117. About 50 percent of orangutans have broken bones. This is because they frequent fall from trees.

118. The sun accounts for 99.87 percent of the weight of the solar system.

119. Nearly all calico cats are females. The rare one in three thousand that is male has an extra X chromosome and is thus sterile.

120. The Buddha often portrayed in statues and images is not the same person. The real Buddha was extremely thin as a result of self-deprivation.

121. A physician has estimated that the phosphorous content in the human body is sufficient to make 220 matchheads.

122. It's impossible to sneeze with your eyes open. When you sneeze, you blink. While the exact reason is not entirely certain, it might to protect our eyes from our snot.

123. Rabbits have almost 360-degree vision, which means they can see in nearly all directions at the same time.

124. Soccer is played in more countries than any other sport.

125. Oddly, right in the center of a hurricane there is an area of total calm where there is no wind at all. This is known as the eye of the storm.

126. Nerves in your body can be as thin as a strand of hair or about as thick as your thumb.

127. Platypuses and spiny anteaters are the only mammals without a belly button.

128. The Pacific Ocean spans a larger area than the combined land surfaces of the entire Earth.

129. An apple, onion, and potato all share the same taste, and their distinct flavors result from their smell.

To prove this, try pinching your nose and taking a bite from each; they will all taste sweet.

130. Two people in Suffolk, England, played chess non-stop for a period of 101 hours.

131. Alaska, the 49th state of the United States, was formerly part of Russian territory. The U.S. acquired it from Russia in 1867 for $7,200,000, a bargain at less than $5 per square kilometer!

132. The biggest ever choir, consisting of 121,440 singers, performed at an event orgainsed by The Art of Living in India in 2011.

133. If you lived on planet Mercury, you could celebrate your "birthday every 88 days, since it takes 88 Earth-days for Mercury to orbit the Sun.

134. While the United States comprises around 4.4% of the world's population, it detains about 22% of the prisoners in the world.

135. In Japan, there's an island named, appropriately enough, Rabbit Island that is exclusively inhabited by bunnies.

136. Fevers have a beneficial role as the increased temperature can potentially eliminate vulnerable bacteria and viruses, and it may also enhance the activity of white blood cells.

137. Chickens are among the world's most embarrassingly poor aviators, with the longest recorded chicken flight lasting only thirteen seconds.

138. Scientists can analyze the ancient atmosphere, dating back around 800,000 years, using the air trapped in ice bubbles collected in Antarctica.

139. The Dogon people use fried onions as a perfume. They rub them all over their body due to their belief that the scent is so attractive.

140. Tigers' night vision is six times better than that of humans.

141. Benjamin Franklin was the youngest son of a youngest son of a youngest son of a youngest son.

142. Every minute, 41,000 dead skin cells leave your epidermis. This process results in an annual loss of up to 4.5 kg (10 pounds) from your body! A significant portion of household dust is in fact consists of dead skin cells.

143. Amazon initially operated under the name Cadabra.com and it only sold books.

144. James Morris had "elastic skin," and could pull the skin of his chest up to the top of his head and stretch his cheeks eight inches out from the side of his face.

145. If you were to place all the blood vessels in your body end to end, they would form a line about 96,000 km (60,000 miles) long.

146. The world's number one producer and consumer of fresh pork is China.

147. To match the strength of a bee, a man would need to be able to pull three lorries, each weighing ten tons.

148. Nuthatches, a type of climbing bird, walk headfirst down a tree.

149. Eyeglasses were invented by the Chinese. Marco Polo reported numerous pairs being worn by them as early as 1275, which is 500 years before the art of lens grinding developed in the West.

150. A Ukrainian craftsman, using a powerful microscope, stitched together the fibers of a spider's web to create a twelve-page book.

151. Food travels through your esophagus at a speed of about one inch (2.5 cm) a second.

152. The amount of heat generated by a human body in a day is enough to power a light bulb for a day and a half.

153. China was the first country to introduce paper money in 812, but it wasn't until 1661 that a Swedish bank issued banknotes.

154. Deer urine can turn blue when they become dehydrated in the winter.

155. During the initial 2 billion years of its existence, Earth had no life on it at whatsoever.

156. It takes about 8 minutes and 19 seconds for sunlight to travel from the sun to Earth. Hence, when we see the sun, we are seeing its position as it was 8 minutes and 19 seconds ago.

157. There are at least 100,000 chemical reactions going on in a normal human brain every second.

158. The longest recorded lifespan of a slug is eighteen months.

159. In Iceland, certain areas have hot springs rising beneath glaciers through the Earth's crust - so it is possible to take a hot bath in a cave made of ice!

160. The name Santa Claus is a corruption of the Dutch dialect name for Saint Nicholas Sint Klass.

161. Dinosaurs likely had a lifespan ranging from 80 to 300 years. Scientists estimated this by examining the structure of their bones.

162. The microwave was invented in the 1940s when a researcher noticed a chocolate bar in his pocket had melted after walking by a radar tube.

163. There are more pyramids in Peru than there are in Egypt.

164. Trump gained the nickname "The Donald" when his Czechoslovakian wife Ivana referred to him as such in an interview.

165. Vatican City, with an area of just 44 hectares, is the world's smallest country. Eight Vaticans could fit inside New York's Central Park.

166. To fly like a bird, we would need wings as big as dinner tables!

167. Though now a toy, the kaleidoscope was originally invented in 1816 to aid textile designers.

168. Sloths can swim three times faster than they can move on land and can remain underwater for up to 40 minutes.

169. A plastic container is estimated to resist decomposition for up to 50,000 years.

170. The fingerprints of any two individuals in the world are never exactly the same. This fact is used to identify criminals.

171. The Tanzanian parasitic wasp holds the title for the world's smallest winged insect. It's smaller than the eye of a housefly.

172. Norman, a French sheepdog, set a world record for scooter riding by covering 100 feet in only 21 seconds. He can ride a bike, too.

173. The front, back, and sides of the tongue have most of the taste buds. The middle has virtually no taste sensation.

174. In 1060, England minted a coin in the shape of a clover. By breaking off the four leaves, the owner could use them as separate coins.

175. Our nearest star neighbor is around 40,230,000 kilometers (25,000,000 miles) away.

176. An Australian man, through over 1,100 blood donations, has saved more than two million babies. His blood contains a unique combination of antibodies used in the treatment of Rhesus disease.

177. Istanbul, a city in Turkey, is situated on both the continents of Asia and Europe.

178. Giraffes are known for their considerable sleep time, averaging about fifteen hours within a twenty-four-hour period. Interestingly, they manage to hide their rest as they only sleep while standing up.

179. The longest recorded nose, measuring 19 centimeters, belonged to a person named Thomas

Wedders.

180. As a small boy, Roald Dahl made a pilgrimage to see Beatrix Potter. When he got there, all she said was: 'Well, you've seen her. Now, buzz off!'

181. Your likelihood of being murdered statistically stands at one in twenty thousand.

182. Parrots, the most famous among talking birds, seldom develop a vocabulary exceeding twenty words.

183. If all the roots of the pumpkin plant were laid end to end, the total length of the root system would extend for 24 kilometers.

184. The Amazon rainforest, known as the "lungs of the Earth," is home to a staggering 400 billion trees spanning more than 16,000 species.

185. 'Bow-wow,' 'Ding-dong,' and 'Pooh-pooh' are all names for different theories explaining the origin of language.

186. In 2014, Psy's "Gangnam Style" music video achieved the milestone of being the first video to exceed two billion views on YouTube. This forced YouTube to upgrade from a thirty-two-bit to a sixty-four-bit integer system.

187. On August 26, 1960, at Vostok in Antarctica the temperature dropped to an all-time low of —88.3°C (—

126°F')

188. A 200-year-old Tibetan cheese was sold at auction for $1,513, in 1993.

189. The first animal to ask an existential question was a parrot named Alex, who asked about his color and learned that he was gray.

190. In April 1906, a head-on collision took place in Redruth, Cornwall. So what? The accident was between the only two cars existing in the town at the time.

191. The oldest known rocks on the earth's surface are nearly 4.2 billion years old.

192. In the early days of cinema, movies were filmed on a nitrate film base, which is extremely flammable. This led to numerous incidents of movie house fires caused by the film catching fire in the projector.

193. The network of arteries, veins, and small capillaries in your circulatory system extends to a length of around 60,000 to 100,000 miles (96,560 to 161,000 km).

194. Snails can sleep for three years without waking up.

195. The ice-cream cheeseburger, featured at the state fair in - Florida, U.S.A., has a scoop of fried ice cream for one of its layers.

196. The Austrian Alps cover 62 percent of the total land area in Austria.

197. In the early 1900s, sunglasses were referred to as "sun cheaters" in America, with "cheaters" being a term for eyeglasses during that period.

198. Canada boasts the highest number of lakes in the world, with 9% of its land area covered by freshwater.

199. Oddly, a wind blowing at 75 miles per hour exerts nine times more force than a wind moving at 25 miles per hour.

200. Although they are not the largest, fastest, or biggest animals, only humans have the ability to run for long distances.

201. A coin flipped will land on its edge about once in every 6,000 flips.

202. There are more than 7,000 different Caribbean islands, but only about 2% of them are inhabited.

203. The size of an ostrich egg is comparable to that of a watermelon, measuring 20 cm in length, 15 cm in diameter, and weighing 1.78 kg. It can yield Omelettes for eight persons.

204. The technical definition of horsepower is the

power needed to lift 33,000 pounds by one foot in one minute. According to this definition, the average horse has only about 0.7 horsepower.

205. The letter E is the most frequently used letter in the English language, followed by A and then R. It can be remembered by the word EAR. Conversely, the letter Z is the least common.

206. Ancient Egyptians had a deep affection for cats and would express mourning for a cat's death by shaving off their eyebrows.

207. Squirrels typically have a longer lifespan in captivity, lasting fifteen to twenty years, as opposed to the wild where they often survive only about one year.

208. Chewing on leather can provide nourishment to sustain life for a short time.

209. The River Nile has frozen over only two occasions in living memory: first in the ninth century and later in the eleventh century.

FACTS 210-314

210. Mao Tse-tung's Little Red Book became the second-best-selling book in the world, right after the Bible, due to Mao's directive that every person in China should possess a copy.

211. A woman in Shrewsbury, England, once broke a rib by sneezing.

212. In 1910, a man called Morton Norbury was killed after an argument over who had the most handsome moustache.

213. Box jellyfish have eyes but lack a brain.

214. The first remote control, known as Lazy Bones, was introduced by Zenith in 1950 and was connected to the television set via a wire.

215. In 1910, the eccentric Princess Radziwill of Poland opted for a chariot pulled by a lion and a leopard, believing they would be swifter than horses. Unfortunately, they proved otherwise.

216. When you sneeze, all your bodily functions briefly pause, including your heartbeat.

217. Mrs. Ann Hodges of Sylacauga, Alabama, USA, was the first person recorded to be injured by a meteorite on November 30, 1954. A 4 kg meteorite broke through her house's roof, striking her arm and bruised her hip.

218. The term "tanks" originated when the vehicles were first transported to France. For security reasons, they were packaged in crates which were supposed to contain water tanks. This mislabeling led to the adoption of the name "tanks."

219. The grey whale isn't really grey. It's black and only seems grey when viewed from a distance.

220. The fastest growing creature on Earth is the blue whale. From the time it begins growing to full growth it increases up to 30,000 million times in size.

221. Humans have only explored a small fraction, less than 5 percent, of the oceans.

222. In Germany, it is considered very bad table manners to cut potatoes with a knife; it should be done using a fork.

223. Charlie Chaplin anonymously participated in a Charlie Chaplin look-alike competition and didn't win any prizes at all!

224. The world's largest salt flat is the Salar de Uyuni in Bolivia, covering about 4050 square miles. It was once a lake that evaporated, leaving a thick salt crust.

225. It would take you nearly six months to drive a car from earth to the moon at a speed of 60 miles

(97/km/h) an hour.

226. It takes 24 hours for a tiny newborn swan to peck its way out of its shell.

227. The liver has the remarkable ability to regenerate even after sustaining colossal damage. Liver transplants are feasible, as a person can donate half of their liver, and the portion that is taken will grow back!

228. The shoelace was invented in England in 1790. Prior to that, shoes were commonly fastened using buckles.

229. King Pepi II of Egypt employed a unique method to ward off bothersome flies; he maintained a supply of naked slaves smeared with honey.

230. Forty-seven Bibles are sold or distributed throughout the world every minute of the day.

231. The penalty for stealing a rabbit in 19th century England was seven years in prison.

232. During the 1920s, when insulin was still derived from animals, it required 10,000 pounds of pig pancreases to produce one pound of concentrated insulin.

233. The word "Ludo" originated from the Latin term 'ludo,' which means 'I play.'

234. Chocolate, bread, and ice cream are the preferred foods among women, while men tend to favor red meat, pizza, and potatoes.

235. Swatting a fly is challenging due to its exceptional vision, allowing it to see in 4,000 different directions simultaneously! Their eyes are made up of that number of different facets (or lenses).

236. Diamonds were formed 1 billion years ago at depths of around one hundred miles beneath the Earth's surface.

237. The vending machine has been around since the time of Christ. The first vending machine, created by the Greek scientist Hero in the 1st century B.C., was a coin-operated dispenser for holy water.

238. Fire trucks were originally painted red because that was the cheapest color.

239. There's a Maine lobster vending game where one can spend three dollars to have fifteen seconds to use a mechanical claw to grab a live lobster from a tank in the machine.

240. The average American drives around 627,000 miles (1,009,059 kilometers) throughout their lifetime, which is equivalent to completing 25 trips around the world.

241. During eight hours of sleep, the average person

changes his position around 35 times.

242. In New Zealand, scientists observed yellow jacket wasps picking up ants and moving them to a new location to prevent competition for the same food.

243. A couple in Michigan received a package at their home and were shocked to discover a liver and an ear inside! The intended destination for these body parts was supposed to be a nearby research laboratory.

244. One out of every three English males between the ages of seventeen and thirty-five was killed in World War I.

245. Around the world, excluding desert and polar regions, there are approximately one thousand different species of bats, constituting about 25% of all mammals on Earth.

246. The starfish has an eye on the end of each arm.

247. The movie adaptation of Popeye was filmed in Malta, leading to the renaming of a village on the island as Popeye Village.

248. The United States discontinued the two-dollar bill in 1966 due to a superstition claiming it brought bad luck. However, it was reissued in 1976.

249. The record for the highest number of children born to a single woman: 69.

250. During the 1500s, brides carried bouquets of flowers to hide their body odor, which has evolved into the modern tradition of carrying a bouquet during weddings.

251. The Defence Budget of Andorra in 1972 was the equivalent of £2.

252. Due to the Earth's rotation, throwing an object westward allows it to cover a greater distance compared to throwing it in other directions.

253. Valencia is the name of the third largest city in both Venezuela and Spain! The cities also each have around 1.8 million inhabitants in their metropolitan areas.

254. The tail of a snow leopard is nearly equal in length to its body.

255. There is a legal obligation in Milan, Italy, to smile at all times, with a few exceptions like hospital visits and funerals.

256. It seems as though turtles and snails have endless time in the world. A turtle moves at a pace of 0.25 mph (0.4 km/h), covering 435 yards (400 m) in an hour. If a snail is really in a hurry and gives its best effort, it can travel at 0.03 mph (0.05 km/h), covering 55 yards (50 m) in one hour.

257. Over 7,000 Americans die each year, and 1,500,000 suffer injuries due to the poor handwriting of doctors.

258. The human brain has a storage capacity that exceeds 4 terabytes.

259. The speed at which the earth orbits around the sun is about eight times faster than that at which a bullet leaves a gun.

260. Female platypuses don't have teats. Instead, they release milk through pores in the skin, and the young lick up the milk collected in skin folds.

261. About 25% of your brain is dedicated to controlling your eyes.

262. The original title of "Alice's Adventures in Wonderland" (1865) was "Alice's Adventures Underground."

263. All the paint on the Eiffel Tower weighs as much as 10 elephants. It undergoes repainting every 7 years without shutting down for the public.

264. In the absence of gravity's effects, astronauts can experience a height increase of up to two inches in space.

265. A meteor that fell in Siberia in 1908 resulted in the death of about 1,500 reindeer.

266. The longest earthworm in the world is found in South Africa. In 1937, one was found to be an impressive 6.7 meters (22 feet) long and 20 millimeters (0.78 inches) in diameter.

267. When a man meets a cow in Pine Island, Minnesota, he is required by law to remove his hat.

268. The number of stars in the universe is estimated to be more than the total number of grains of sand on Earth.

269. The Pacific Ocean is home to the largest waves, reaching heights of up to 34 meters.

270. Some astronomers believe that Pluto's unusual and unpredictable orbit suggests it might have originated as a moon of Neptune that eventually became detached.

271. A criminal was arrested and found guilty in Harlow, Essex, of stealing over 800 Bus-Stop signs.

272. In a 2002 study conducted by Andrew Balmford, it was found that eight-year-old British children could accurately recognize 80% of various Pokémon species, while their identification rate for common types of wild animals was only 50%.

273. To absorb the carbon dioxide emitted by an average car in a year, around one acre of forest is needed.

274. For the first time in history, more species are being lost every year than found.

275. German tennis star Sabine Lisicki's serve has been clocked at 131 miles an hour (210.8 km/h) - that's faster than a speeding train!

276. Dolphins sleep with one of its eyes open.

277. The Dutch town of Abcoude is the only town in the world whose name start with the letters ABC.

278. The Arctic fox frequently follows the polar bear, feeding on the remains of its prey.

279. The NASDAQ stock exchange in New York experienced a complete outage for a day in December 1987 when a squirrel burrowed through a telephone line.

280. Soybeans are used in making glue, paint, plastics, and explosives.

281. Cleopatra, the ancient queen of Egypt, was actually of entirely Greek origin, not Egyptian.

282. In Japan, you have the option to enjoy ice cream with the flavor of ox tongue.

283. The East Alligator River in the Northern

Territory of Australia was incorrectly named, as it contains crocodiles instead of alligators.

284. Two words in the English language contain the vowels a, e, i, o, u, in that order: abstemious and facetious.

285. During the American War of Independence (1775-78), inflation reached extreme levels in America, with the price of wheat surging by 14,000 percent and the price of beef skyrocketing by 33,000 percent.

286. Cats lack the ability to taste sweet things.

287. During the Battle of the Oranges festival in Ivrea, Italy, held every February, residents engage in throwing more than 400 tons of oranges at each other.

288. Nuclear fuel rods used in nuclear reactors are used for five years. Following this, they are placed in water pools for cooling, a process that can extend for up to twenty years.

289. Over 68 percent of Earth's freshwater is frozen in glaciers.

290. Australia is home to a mountain known as Mt. Disappointment and another mountain named Mt. Terrible.

291. Penguins can drink saltwater because of a gland in their throat that eliminates the salt from the water.

292. One pufferfish carries sufficient poison to kill 30 individuals.

293. The oldest cockroach fossil dates back approximately 280 million years, indicating that cockroaches existed 80 million years before the appearance of the first dinosaurs.

294. On average, individuals consume about one ton of food and drink annually.

295. While filming Cleopatra, Elizabeth Taylor's husband at the time, Eddie Fisher, received a daily payment of $1500 to ensure she arrived at work punctually.

296. A tiger's skin beneath its striped fur is also striped, and each tiger has a unique pattern of stripes, making no two tigers identical.

297. Statistically speaking, being the President of the United States is considered the most dangerous job in America, with approximately 9% of presidents having been killed while in office.

298. Qatar is the only country that begins with a Q and Iraq is the only country that ends with one.

299. The Toda people in India are prohibited by their religion from crossing any kind of bridge.

300. The first video camera recorder, introduced in 1956, had a price tag of $50,000 and was as large as a piano.

301. Before football referees started using whistles in 1878, they used to rely on waving a handkerchief.

302. The ancient Romans favored a concoction of boiled vinegar and goat feces as their energy drink. Charioteers believed it enhanced their performance in the arena.

303. The most common name in the world in Mohammed.

304. Women's hearts, on average, beat 78 times per minute, while men's hearts beat 70 times per minute.

305. The cougar, or the mountain lion, has over 40 names in English alone, earning it the Guinness World Record for the animal with the most names.

306. The honeybee kills more people world-wide than all the poisonous snakes put together.

307. During the summer months between May and July in the Faroe Islands, the nights are so well illuminated that lighthouses are turned off.

308. Among the Seven Wonders of the Ancient World, only the Pyramids of Egypt is still in existence, while the others have deteriorated and disappeared. The primary factor contributing to the pyramid's enduring presence is its exceptional ability to withstand the effects of gravity.

309. Ants and humans are the only two species that engage in warfare against members of their own species.

310. The odds of having a car accident are 70 percent higher in the rain.

311. Pepsi introduced a morning soft drink named Pepsi AM in 1989, but it didn't last long on the market.

312. In Thailand, kite-flying is an important sport with organized teams, umpires, official rules, and a national championship for teams.

313. Fish dwelling at depths exceeding 800 meters below the ocean surface don't have eyes because the extreme darkness renders them unnecessary.

314. The Nobel Prize, a highly esteemed awards across diverse fields, has an unexpected origin. Alfred Nobel, the Swedish inventor renowned for his invention of dynamite, established it.

Facts 315 – 419

315. Astronomers identified the fastest star in the galaxy in 2005. It was zooming through the Milky Way at more than 3.9 million kilometers per hour.

316. Cats that don't interact with humans by the time they're 10 weeks old will retain a lifelong fear of them.

317. Rennet, a commonly used substance for curdling milk and making cheese, is taken from the inner lining of a calf's fourth stomach.

318. Explorer Ibn Battuta (1304-1368) traveled 75,000 miles on foot, by camel, and by ship during his lifetime, which is equivalent to three circumnavigations of the Earth.

319. There are 19 languages on Earth with only one speaker left.

320. Pablo Escobar, the drug lord, once burned $2 million in cash in a single night to provide warmth for his family.

321. One of the most powerful female pirates was Madame Cheng. After her husband's death in 1807, she assumed his command and expanded it into 1,800 boats and 80,000 pirates.

322. A "coward" was originally a boy who took care

of cows.

323. A hippopotamus has a unique transparent membrane covering its eyes, functioning like goggles to provide clear vision underwater.

324. Owls possess the ability to rotate their heads fully, allowing them to see objects directly behind them.

325. The coldest inhabited place in the world is the Siberian village of Qymyakon, where temperatures have reached -96°F (-71°C).

326. Every month, you lose approximately three-quarters of a pound of skin, which is equivalent to the weight of a small loaf of bread.

327. In Egypt, if you can drive forwards and backwards just 6 metres you can pass your driving test.

328. At their nearest point, the United States and Russia are less than two miles apart.

329. Saturn is surrounded by huge rings. They are sufficient to fit around 400 Earths. The rings are made of space dust and relatively thin, spanning just a few kilometers.

330. The human brain constitutes about 2% of the entire body weight, yet it consumes about 20% of the body's overall energy.

331. Although Michael Jackson is most famous for popularizing the moonwalk, the dance move had been performed years earlier by entertainers such as Sammy Davis, Jr., Cab Calloway, and Fred Astaire.

332. The northern leopard frog swallows its prey using its eyes; it utilizes them to assist in pushing food down its throat by retracting them into its head.

333. The world's population is increasing by 2.4 people a second.

334. When honey is swallowed, it enters the blood stream within a period of about 20 minutes.

335. A human hair laid on a bar of steel and then passed through a cold rolling mill would leave an imprint on the face of the steel.

336. Your sense of hearing is better when you're hungry compared to when you've just eaten.

337. Umami is the fifth taste sensation, identified relatively recently, characterized by a savory flavor attributed to the presence of glutamate, an amino acid. It is commonly found in foods such as tomatoes, meat, cheese, mushrooms, and others.

338. Very small amounts of cyanide, a lethal poison, are present in apple seeds.

339. In Colonial America, it was trendy to wear wigs, crafted not only from human hair but also from the hair of horses, goats, and even yaks.

340. The longest non-talking film ever made was Andy Warhol's Sleep. It consists solely of a man sleeping for eight hours.

341. Thomas Jefferson, John Adams, and James Monroe all died on July 4th. Jefferson and Adams died at practically the same minute of the same day.

342. Leonardo da Vinci had the ability to write with one hand while drawing with the other. You try.

343. The sentence "the quick brown fox jumps over the lazy dog" uses every letter of the alphabet.

344. Sharks and rays are the only animals known to man that don't get cancer. Researchers attribute this trait to the absence of bones and the presence of cartilage in their bodies.

345. An adult walrus eats approximately 3000 clams a day.

346. The 1906 San Francisco earthquake had the seismic force equivalent to 12,000 Hiroshima nuclear bombs.

347. On December 7, 1968, Richard Dodd returned a library book that had been borrowed by his great-grandfather in 1823 from the University of Cincinnati Medical Library.

348. If the coils of a French horn were straightened out, the instrument would be 22 feet long.

349. Electricity travels at the speed of light, covering about 186,000 miles per second.

350. The president of the World Chess Federation is of the opinion that the world will face destruction by aliens unless more chess is played.

351. Boeing's Everett Plant, designed for the production of the 747 Jumbo Jet, is the world's biggest factory. The factory covers an area equivalent to 40 American football pitches!

352. Birds practise their songs quietly in private before they perform them in public.

353. Garlic that has been stored in oil for too long can result in the formation of the highly toxic poison botulism.

354. There are around 6,500 different languages spoken worldwide.

355. Bhutan is the only country with a carbon-negative status, meaning it absorbs more carbon dioxide than it produces. Around 72% of the country remains covered by forests.

356. The number of Lego bricks sold each would stretch around Earth more than 18 times.

357. Google was named after the mathematical term "googol," which denotes the number 1 followed by 100 zeros.

358. The remote Russian island Яя (Ya Ya) was found in 2013 by a cargo helicopter. The crew shouted 'Я, я!' – 'Me, me!' ('I saw it first, I saw it first!') and that became the island's name.

359. In 1984, on the Upper East Side of New York, Todd Berenger opened a restaurant named "Twins," where the staff consisted of twenty-nine sets of identical twins.

360. When you make contact with an object, a message travels from your fingers to your brain at a speed of 93 mph - as fast as a speeding train.

361. Contrary to the phrase "crocodile tears," crocodiles do not actually cry or produce tears.

362. A scientist from the Museum of Natural History in Paris claims that snails have a sense of direction when they begin their journey but are so slow that they may forget their destination along the way.

363. Termites chew at a faster rate when exposed to loud and fast music.

364. The biggest iceberg ever seen measured more than 200 miles (320 km) in length and 60 miles (96 km) in width.

365. It's possible to lead a cow upstairs but not downstairs.

366. The shortest war in world history took place between Great Britain and Zanzibar on August 27, 1896, with a duration of just 38 minutes.

367. The Amazon River contributes about 20% of the total freshwater that floods into the oceans from rivers.

368. A trillion metric tons of the world's water evaporates each day in the sun. Fortunately, it all comes down again when it rains!

369. In the USA, domestic cats are responsible for the estimated death of around one billion wild birds annually.

370. The sensitivity of human eyes is remarkable; under clear moonless nights, an individual seated on a mountain peak can see a match being struck as far as 50 miles away.

371. Upon learning of Prince Charles's birth, the American people expressed their congratulations by sending a gift of 1.5 tons of nappies to the Queen.

372. The Amazon rainforest produces one fifth of the world's oxygen.

373. The age of a dolphin can be determined by counting the rings in its teeth, similar to the way tree rings indicate age.

374. In December 1961, it was found that a painting by Matisse in New York's Museum of Modern Art was hanging upside down.

375. The first successful electric elevator was installed in the Demarest Building in New York City, in 1889.

376. Cicero voiced the famous words "Ask not what your country can do for you, but rather what you can do for your country" two thousand years before John F. Kennedy made the statement.

377. Sloths are good swimmers; using a modified dog paddle technique, they can move in water up to three times faster than they move on land.

378. The sun loses four million tons of mass every second.

379. Cows that are given names produce more milk than those without names, as shown by a 2009 study.

380. The inner lining of your small intestine is around 2,700 square feet (251 square meters), which is nearly equivalent to the size of a basketball court.

381. Bruce Lee had the ability to perform a push-up with just two fingers, relying on his thumb and forefinger for support.

382. Million Dollar Point is an are in the Pacific where the U.S. military disposed of its equipment after World War II by dumping it into the ocean, as it was more cost-effective than transporting it back home.

383. Albert Einstein's last words will never be known. He spoke them in German, and his nurse didn't speak any German.

384. The bald eagle is not truly bald; its head is covered with white feathers, creating the appearance of baldness when seen from a distance.

385. In the U.S., black is the traditional color worn to signify mourning, while in China, people typically opt for white dress when attending a funeral.

386. In 1817, there was an unusual event in Appin, Scotland, where thousands of small herring fell from the sky. The fish had been swept aloft by strong air currents in rain clouds.

387. Only humans and monkeys, among mammals, have the ability to distinguish colors.

388. The force of your heartbeat is strong enough to shoot water up to a height of six feet (1.8 m).

389. Neil Armstrong did not say "one small step for man" when he stepped onto the Moon. Instead, he claimed to have said "one small step for a man," and audio analysis confirms his statement. It has been misquoted all these years.

390. Any whole number decreased by the sum of its digits will leave a remainder that can be divided by 9.

391. Michael Phelps, if considered a country, would surpass 97 nations, securing the 35th position on the all-time Olympic gold medal list.

392. 50% of all bank robberies are done on Fridays.

393. The 10,000 species of birds alive today make up less than 1% of all the bird species that have ever existed.

394. New York is considered the most linguistically diverse city in the world, with experts estimating that it is home to about 800 languages.

395. In Bali, dragonflies are eaten with coconut milk, ginger, garlic, shallots - or just plain-grilled and crispy.

396. In ancient China, dinosaur bones were believed to be the remnants of dragons, and they were pulverized for use in medicines and magical potions.

397. At a rate of one second per person, it would take more than a century to count the population of the world.

398. Al-Jazari, an Arab inventor, created the first robots around AD 1200!

399. During World War II, nine thousand bombs had to be dropped on a target to achieve a 90 percent probability of hitting it.

400. All the stars in the Milky Way completes a rotation around the center of galaxy every two hundred million years.

401. Denmark's national flag, showcasing a white cross on a red background, has been in continuous use for nearly 800 years, making it the oldest national flag still in use.

402. Scientists in the United Kingdom have developed a device that can turn urine into electricity.

403. Humans used to think the Stone Age was what made us special. But chimpanzees also experienced a Stone Age of their own. For around 4,000 years, they have been using stone tools to crack nuts.

404. Slugs have around 27,000 teeth.

405. The average golf ball has 336 dimples. These tiny craters make the ball more aerodynamic, enabling it to travel longer distances, at higher speeds, and improving the precision of the shot.

406. There are 170,000,000,000,000,000, 000,000,000 ways to play the ten opening moves in a game of chess.

407. The initial aerial battles in World War I came to be called "dogfights" because, similar to two dogs pursuing one another, each plane aimed to position itself behind the other.

408. The chameleon's tongue, which always hits its prey, can be stretched to more than twice the length of the chameleon's body.

409. During the Middle Ages, pepper was used for bartering, and its value often surpassed that of gold.

410. Grasshopper glacier in Montana, USA contains layers of grasshoppers preserved in ice.

411. Sunlight is unable to penetrate the ocean beyond a depth of 665 feet, so everything else beneath that is in permanent darkness.

412. Dinosaurs disappeared from Earth prior to the formation of the Alps or the Rocky Mountains.

413. Charlie Chaplin was stolen from his own grave

and his body held for a ransom of 600,000 francs.

414. It takes one thousandth of a second for a sound to travel from one ear on your head to the other.

415. Guam has the highest concentration of snakes in the world, with some areas having up to 12,000 snakes per square mile.

416. In the mid-seventeenth century, a man from Lincolnshire was put on stocks for two hours for publicly kissing his wife on a Sunday, because it was strictly forbidden to do such a thing on a Sunday.

417. Not all the light we see in the sky at night are stars, some of them are planets.

418. The fastest moon in our solar system completes an orbit around Jupiter every seven hours, moving at a speed of 70,400 miles per hour.

419. France passed a "right to disconnect" law in 2017, enabling individuals to disregard emails received outside regular business hours.

FACTS 420 – 525

420. The fastest camera in the world captures images using lasers at a rate of one image per nanosecond. That's one image every billionth of a second.

421. Since 2007, residents in the small European country of Estonia can cast their votes for political leaders using their computers.

422. There are chemicals called arsole, urantae, fucol, dogcollarane, apatite and cummingtonite.

423. African American Rosa Parks started a mass civil rights movement in 1955 when she was arrested for refusing to give up her bus seat to a white man.

424. Elephants sing to each other, but you can't hear their songs. They're sung too low for the human ear to hear.

425. The Mountain Devil, a lizard-like creature that lives in Australia, never drinks. Instead, it absorbs small dew droplets through its skin.

426. Shakespeare invented 1,700 words that are still part of our vocabulary today.

427. During a speech in 1961, President John F. Kennedy delivered a record-breaking 327 words per minute.

428. Tonga, a country in the South Pacific, once issued a stamp in the shape of a banana.

429. Belcher's sea snake holds the title of the most venomous snake, with its poison being 100 times more potent than that of the most dangerous land snake, the western taipan in Australia.

430. 100,000 TONS (90,718) of bubble gum is chewed, worldwide, every year.

431. The combined volume of water drunk by humans throughout history would be sufficient to create a layer less than three millimeters deep covering the Earth's oceans.

432. Oysters are initially born as males but have the ability to switch their gender back and forth in response to environmental factors.

433. The British crown jewels are currently housed at the Tower of London, which has served various purposes over time, including being a zoo, observatory, mint, and prison.

434. South American monkeys have tails that can grip. They use their tails like a fifth limb as they swing through the trees.

435. Thomas Edison, the inventor of reliable electric light bulbs, had a fear of darkness. Reportedly, all the lights in his house were kept on when he died.

436. A female pigeon requires the presence of another pigeon to lay an egg, and if none is available, her own reflection in a mirror will do.

437. The model for the Indian head penny was the engraver's daughter.

438. Lightning is always seen before thunder because the speed of light is much faster than the speed of sound.

439. In 1974, surfing clubs in Brisbane, Australia, discovered 250 pairs of dentures lost by swimmers and surfers on the Gold Coast in Queensland.

440. Wolffia angusta, the smallest flowering plant, is incredibly tiny, with two flowering plants small enough to fit inside this letter "o".

441. There are more than 50 million Minecraft users. That's a number larger than the entire population of Spain.

442. The great ancient Roman leader Julius Caesar (100-44 BC), who conquered many lands, was said to have been captured by pirates when on his way to school as a boy, but charmed his way to freedom.

443. Smokey the cat holds the world record for the loudest purr made by a domestic cat. The sound of her purr, when recorded, surpasses the noise level of a vacuum cleaner.

444. Even highly intelligent individuals use only about one percent of the available vocabulary in the English language during their conversations.

445. Pablo Picasso finished his first artwork, "Le Picador," when he was only nine years old.

446. The number 526,315,789,473,684,210 is the most persistent number mathematically. No matter how many times you multiply it by any number, the original digits will always reappear in the result.

447. The eighteenth-century name for a butcher was a 'fleshflogger'.

448. The surname Smith is the most common name in the English language, followed by Johnson in second place.

449. Blood travels a considerable distance within the human body. There are about 60,000 miles of blood vessels in the human body. The heart, tirelessly pumping, pumps around 2,000 gallons of blood through these vessels daily.

450. Queen Victoria's first act after being crowned was to move her bed from her mother's room.

451. A retired teacher who had been experiencing

difficulty breathing for several months was amazed when doctors informed him that a pea plant was sprouting in his lung.

452. The tenrac, a hedgehog-like animal from Madagascar, has twenty-two to twenty-four nipples.

453. In the absence of gravity in space, blood circulation behaves differently. Blood may move upwards towards the head instead of being pulled downwards towards the feet. As a result, astronauts' faces often appear puffy due to increased blood flow during the initial days until their bodies adjust.

454. "Unprosperousness" is the longest word in which no letter occurs only once.

455. Flight recorders and black boxes are stored in the tails of airplanes because this area is deemed the most resilient and likely to withstand a crash.

456. It takes approximately 165 years for Neptune to complete one orbit around the Sun.

457. If you were to remove all the space within the atoms composing a camel, the camel could pass through the eye of a needle.

458. Mosquitoes prefer biting children over adults and blondes over brunettes.

459. A recent study revealed that infants who receive

greater amounts of hugs and physical contact demonstrate more advanced brain development.

460. The longest train ever was over 7.3 kilometres long and contained 660 trucks. It travelled from Saldanha to Sishen in South Africa on 26 August 1989.

461. Florida has more bear-hunters than bears.

462. To find the letter "A" when spelling out numbers, you'd need to count all the way to one thousand.

463. Bhutan was the last country to get the telephone. It did not have one until 1981.

464. Oprah is 'Harpo' backwards. Oprah Winfrey's real name is Orpah (after the sister of Ruth in the Bible) but no one could say or spell it properly so she eventually gave up correcting them.

465. A cow's sweat glands are located in its nose, and similar to human fingerprints, the unique features of a cow's nose can be used for identification purposes.

466. Women from the Asin Kirghiz tribe risk immediate divorce if they speak the names of their husbands.

467. Every day the world's population flushes away 27,000 trees worth of toilet paper.

468. Ten medium-sized potato crisps contain more than one hundred calories.

469. Sea cucumbers have bodies that can reach lengths of 1 meter (3 feet). When cut into pieces, each segment has the potential to regenerate into a new sea cucumber.

470. The Turks call the turkey an "American bird."

471. Galileo lost his sight completely shortly before his death, likely due to his prolonged observation of the sun through his telescope.

472. After death, elephants have been reported to remain standing for some time.

473. It's estimated that parents lose approximately 400 to 750 hours of sleep in the first year after a new baby is born.

474. Sixty-eight percent of professional hockey players have lost at least one tooth.

475. A scientist studying a single rye plant found 13,800,000 rootlets and root hairs, which, if placed end to end, would stretch 387 miles.

476. The Great Wall of China is one of the very few man-made structures that would be visible from the moon.

477. In ancient times, Greeks and Romans used spider webs as bandages. Even today, some believe spider webs have antifungal and antiseptic qualities along with vitamin K, which aids in clotting.

478. The term "school" originates from the Greek word "Skhol," which means leisure time or time for spiritual exercises.

479. The first steam-powered submarine was named the Resurgam, translating to 'I will rise again,' yet it sank almost immediately after its launch.

480. The amount of ice lost in Antarctica every year would be suffice to provide each person on Earth 1,360,000 ice cubes.

481. The 63-letters-long German word Rindfleischetikettierungsuberwachungsaufgabeniibertra gungsgesetz is no longer in use - not because of its length, but because it referred to a law about beef that was repealed.

482. Earth's atmosphere is, proportionally, thinner than the skin of an apple.

483. An orange tree can produce oranges for over a century. The renowned "Constable Tree," an orange tree transported to France in 1421, lived and bore fruit for 473 years.

484. At the onset of World War I, the United States

Air Force consisted of only fifty men.

485. According to research conducted by Rothamsted Research, fertile farmland can host up to 1,750,000 earthworms per acre. This implies that on a dairy farm, the earthworm population underground could easily outweigh the weight of the livestock above.

486. You may spend up to half of your waking hours day dreaming, according to one study.

487. A single summer on Uranus spans a duration of 21 Earth-years.

488. If you're right-handed, you tend to chew food on the right side of your mouth; if you're left-handed, you tend to chew on the left.

489. Linus Pauling is the only man ever to win two individual Nobel prizes; one for peace, the other for chemistry.

490. In Denmark, if someone offers you carrots to eat on your last day of staying with them, it means that they don't want you to return anytime soon.

491. In the United States, more Frisbee discs are sold each year than baseballs, basketballs, and footballs combined.

492. If every egg that every insect laid hatched, then grew into an adult insect and lived its natural life span, there would be very little room for any other animal in the world.

493. The original name given to the butterfly was the 'flutterby'.

494. In Finland, speeding fines are adjusted based on the offender's income. In 2002, a Nokia executive was fined €116,000 for driving 75 kph in a 50 kph zone.

495. For a billion years, the only life on Earth was a kind of slime. Scientists call this period 'the boring billion'.

496. The rest of the Body rots away after death, but bones can endure for thousands of years.

497. Olympic swimmers achieved remarkably fast times while wearing a swimsuit developed with assistance from NASA. It made swimmers so fast that it's now been banned.

498. The remains of birds hit by aeroplanes are known as 'snarge'.

499. Early bubble gum was pink because it was the only food coloring available at the time.

500. In Arabic writing, words are written from right to left, while Arabic numbers are written from left to right. Therefore, Arabic speakers reading texts with a lot of numbers have to read in both directions at once.

501. In Tibet and parts of Nepal the people drink a type of beer made from rice. They call it 'chang'.

502. In southern Germany, there was a superstition that if the youngest child in the household sneezed in bed on a Saturday night, it was believed to bring good luck to the family for the following week.

503. The Carthaginians in the sixth century named Spain "Spania" or "Span," which means "land of rabbits."

504. There are 1,929,770,126,0268,600 possible different colour combinations on a Rubik's Cube.

505. The first-known pizza shop, Port Alba in Naples, opened in 1830 and remains operational to this day.

506. The first video uploaded to YouTube on April 23, 2005, titled "Meet Me at the Zoo". It was 19-second video of a boy explaining that elephants have long tusks.

507. Dinosaurs, some of the most advanced creatures that ever lived on the Earth. They survived for approximately 150 million years, a span seventy-five times longer than the current duration of human existence on the planet.

508. When you are asleep your ear continues to function, but your brain filters out the noise so that you can sleep.

509. The Stonefish of the tropical Pacific Ocean is so poisonous, one touch from the spines on its fins could kill a man.

510. Candlefish is another name for the Eulachon species of fish. Due to the fish's extremely high fat content, it is possible to use the fish as a candle!

511. The oldest water on Earth was discovered 1.5 miles (2.4 km) deep in a Canadian mine. It dates back to between 1 and 2.5 billion years old.

512. To avoid being hit by space junk in 2014 the International Space Station (ISS) had to change orbit three times.

513. Staff at a zoo in Britain had to feed milk by hand to a baby colobus monkey after its mother rejected it, all because the baby had hiccups!

514. On New Year's Day in 1907, Theodore Roosevelt, the American president, greeted 8,513 individuals with a handshake.

515. E is the most frequently used letter in the English language.

516. The Apollo 11 spacecraft had only about 20 seconds of fuel remaining when it landed on the moon!

517. A large blue whale needs three tons of food every day.

518. Sixty per cent of the country of Liechtenstein's GDP is generated from the sale of false teeth.

519. Divorce is prohibited by law in the Philippines. It's the only nation, outside the Vatican, where that is so.

520. A cow in Wellington, New Zealand, was sentenced to two days in jail for grazing on the grass outside the city courthouse.

521. If the moon were placed on the surface of the continental United States, it would stretch from San Francisco to Cleveland, a distance of 2,160 miles.

522. 80% of dreams are about normal things like washing up or being at work.

523. A hundred years ago, a single farmer in the USA could produce sufficient grain to feed 25 individuals. Nowadays, with the help of machinery, one farmer can grow enough to feed 1000 people.

524. One out of every 88 births results in twins. One out of every 512,000 births results in quadruplets.

525. There was a Roman tradition where the leaves of palm trees were laid in the hands of people who won contests, and that's how the underside of our hands came to be known as palms.

Printed in Great Britain
by Amazon

50551493R00042